Lockdown
CAPERS

A couple chronicles the lighter side
of a state-mandated lockdown

JOHN R. PISTACCHI

LUMINARE PRESS
WWW.LUMINAREPRESS.COM

Printed in the United States of America

Cover Design by Kristen Brack

Luminare Press
442 Charnelton St.
Eugene, OR 97401
www.luminarepress.com

LCCN: 2020925069
ISBN: 978-1-64388-569-8

This book is dedicated to the lovely
Martha, my bride and partner for over 50
years, and my children Ann & Michael
who put up with my warped sense of
humor for all these years.

A NOTE FROM THE AUTHOR

This book is intended to bring a smile to readers and maintain a sense of humor as we maneuver through awful times. It is in no way intended to imply that this virus is something to laugh about. I have been personally touched by its very real consequences. One of my dear friends nearly lost her son a few months ago. He is only in his 40's and stayed in the ICU on a ventilator for a period of time. The heroic efforts of the hospital responders saved his life at the last minute. He was actually told that he was their first patient in weeks to come in on a ventilator and leave the hospital alive. Also, one of my uncles perished recently, a victim of Covid-19. It saddens me to think that some people still believe that this pandemic is not real.

Having said that, I still believe that laughter is the best remedy.

To stay in touch with my Parkinson's boxing group during the lockdown, I began posting weekly musings about the situations my wife Martha and I experienced. My readers found them to be helpful and spirit lifting. They encouraged me to share them with a wider audience. So, here we are. I hope you enjoy the book and if it brings you just one smile, I will have accomplished my mission.

THE BEGINNING

On March 19, 2020, California, experiencing a major spike in COVID-19 cases, ordered a lockdown for forty million residents.

On that fateful day, all the people disappeared, and our lives changed forever.

Martha and I hunkered down to adapt to a scary new reality: We were going to be together 24/7, *perhaps forever!*

The extent to which my life changed became obvious upon comparing my April 2019 calendar to my April 2020 calendar.

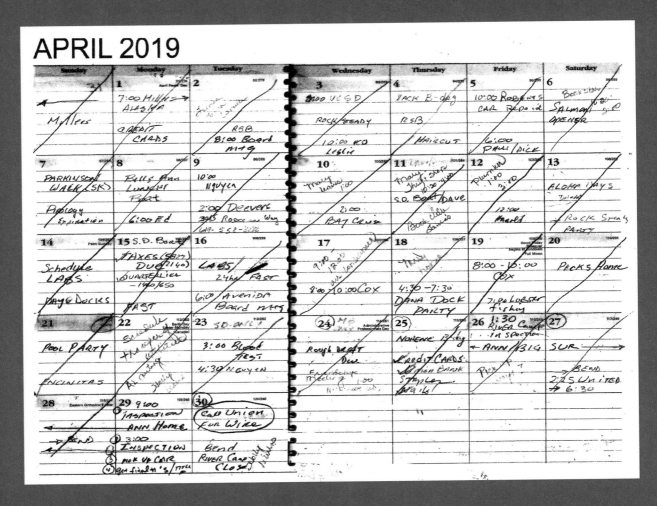

2020 APRIL

SUN	MON	TUE	WED	THU	FRI	SAT
			1 CHECK MAIL	2	3	4 ORDER HBO
5	6 Check for AMAZON BOXES	7	8	9 Look for COSTCO DELIVERY	10	11
12	13	14	15 CHECK MAIL	16	17	18 SHOWER
19 order SHOWTIME	20	21	22	23 RECYCLE AMAZON BOXES	24	25
26	27	28	29 UPGRADE TO 1000 CHANNELS	30		

EARLY OBSERVATION.

Shopping became a choice between venturing outside (looking like terrorists and waiting in long lines) and using delivery services. Guess our choice.

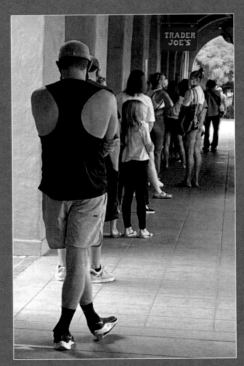

PANDEMIC PROTOCOLS

My adult children adopted an amazing and disciplined protocol for delivered packages. They wear gloves, quarantine the arrivals in the garage for twenty-four hours, and then wipe everything down with a disinfectant.

I, on the other hand, turn into a child on Christmas morning. I see the Amazon truck coming and start running around the house in my jammies (my new dress code) yelling "Presents, presents!" till Martha lets me out.

To do my part and follow the new protocols, I wash my hands thirty to fifty times a day as demonstrated on TV by Doctors Oz and Gupta. I sing the "Happy Birthday" song twice, making sure to use soap and remembering to include my thumbs.

To my horror, during one washing session, I realized I had touched the faucet. I immediately grabbed the nearest disinfectant and sprayed the faucet, but now I had touched the sprayer. I grabbed a towel and wiped down the sprayer, but now I had touched the towel. Exasperated, I laid down on my back, draped the towel over my knees, and holding the spray bottle between my teeth, disinfected the towel. Unfortunately, my arthritis kicked in, and now I can't stand up. This is when my smartwatch (with medical alert capabilities) starts blaring to the world that I have fallen and can't get up and is dialing 911.

HAPPY TRAILS

A favorite activity was a three-mile walk along the edge of the bay, taking photographs of the local wildlife. This wildlife typically consisted of about a million very menacing squirrels.

Squirrels in attack formation

John R. Pistacchi

SQUIRRELY SQUIRRELS

Absolutely no one believes my theory that the trail squirrels are behind this epidemic in an effort to take over the park. I have been watching them, and I'm telling you, they are acting very peculiar. Unfortunately, the trails have been closed off, limiting my ability to monitor their activities.

We Won!! They are all gone, even their dogs.

AMAZON FOLLIES

I confess that I am a serial instant gratification Amazon shopper. You know the type: ordering something the minute it crosses your mind that you need it (a garbage disposal, a tire, a pen, a toothpick, whatever).

During the crisis, however, I am doing my best to use Amazon responsibly. For example, recently, instead of ordering a compact camera battery immediately, I waited very patiently till I had ten other items that I could not live without in my cart (about seven minutes). I clicked on the no hurry button as well as the option that it was OK to wait till items could be combined to minimize packaging. This is how my battery arrived the next day... Amazon, really?

John R. Pistacchi

APRIL OBSERVATIONS

Before Covid, I only had to remember three things when I left the house:

1. my phone
2. my wallet
3. my glasses

Now, I have to remember those three, plus

- my hand sanitizer
- my gloves
- my mask

and, let's see…oh yes, Martha.

~

I just realized that with the advent of email and social media, those "FOREVER" stamps will indeed be with me FOREVER.

I used to ask Martha, "What do you want to watch on TV tonight?" Now, it's, "What do you want to snooze through tonight?"

Forget schools, we need Goodwill centers reopened.

CRY FOR HELP

Martha decides that John's obsession with the squirrels has gone far enough and demands that he get professional help.

John undergoes evaluation

TRAIL CLOSURE WOES

Trail Restricted to pedestrians walking in single file at least 6 feet apart with leashed pets. NO EXCEPTION

Our favorite trail was restricted to *pet walking only* as described by the posted sign at the head of the trail.

Martha solves the problem.

HOARDING MANIA

People are starting to hoard. It seems limited to flour, toilet paper, and cleaning supplies. But, afraid of a run on Martha's favorite treat, I stock up. ...Because you know the saying...*Happy wife, happy life!*

Then, just to play it safe, I store a three-month supply of my essentials.

WORKOUT BLUES

I participate in the national Parkinson's Rock Steady Boxing program to keep my strength and improve my balance. I do this under my fighting name, *Fast Johnny*. Our boxing gym closed down, but luckily, our fabulous coach started daily Zoom classes. We did have to improvise on the equipment, but I found some great hand weights.

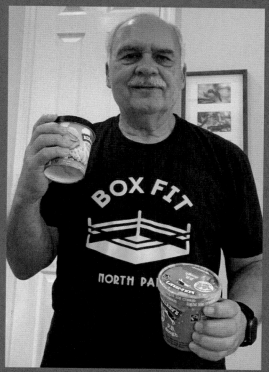

They work amazingly well...and are totally adjustable.

HUNT FOR FLOUR

With massive hoarding going on, it truly became impossible to find flour. I was getting desperate for baked goods. One day, I finally snapped. Before Martha could stop me, I grabbed my mask and sanitizer and bravely visited seven stores...only to find this:

I returned home, jumped online, and discovered this:

Out of Stock   Out of Stock   Out of Stock   Out of Stock

What to do? I considered buying a gun and mask to rob my neighbor…but the waiting period for a mask was too long. Then, I remembered a scribbling on the wall of a Safeway bathroom. It read: "In case of a flour emergency, call this number." I called, and a very hushed voice gave me coordinates to a secret location. That is where I met Sneaky Pete.

Unfortunately, he only accepted sheets of toilet paper for payment. He reluctantly sent me to Shady Bob, who ran a toilet paper exchange.

I got a roll from Shady Bob, but it cost me a can of peaches and a frozen lasagna.

I ran back to Sneaky Pete, but by then, his prices had doubled. Lucky for me, he was having a new client special and was willing to sell me the flour for the original price if I set up an account with a password and signed up for his newsletter. I handed over my precious roll of toilet paper, stuffed the flour under my sweater to avoid an armed robbery, and ran home to finally bake something, anything.

AMAZON TO THE RESCUE

As the flour shortage continued unabated, I searched Amazon. Turns out, they have a *bulk* department. Suddenly, before my eyes, was a plethora of flour brands in twenty-five-, fifty-, one hundred-, and one thousand-pound bags...just waiting to be ordered. I almost wept reading those magic words "in stock." Finally, after giving up on the dangerous underworld for my flour, I was going to be able to bake. I ordered a twenty-five-pound bag. Martha, however, did not share in my enthusiasm for this emergency backup meal source. She pointed out that we had not baked anything requiring flour since the early '70s, and of course, where did I plan on storing all of this GD flour?

EXERCISE PROGRAM UPDATE

My smartwatch (which keeps track of my every movement) just blared an alert telling the world how proud it was of me.

To the sound of watch trumpets, it announced that I had walked thirty-six miles in the past two weeks.

Then the watch broke it down:

Six miles outside

Thirty miles going from the couch to the refrigerator and back.

PASTA MANIA

One morning, I was jolted out of bed by a bright idea. We were going to save a fortune while proving to Martha once and for all that the flour was a smart investment...*We would make our own pasta!*

After all, with store overhead and delivery and price gouging, spaghetti has leaped to what? Maybe $1.29 a pound?

Yep, foolproof, no doubt about it— what could possibly go wrong with this well thought-out enterprise?

Well, here I am so far:

$65................Twenty-five-pound flour bag

$20 ....Flour shipping (FREE on Amazon Prime...but I couldn't wait)

$34............... Two airtight, radiation and bullet proof industrial bins to store the flour

$49................New pasta machine

$17 ....Ravioli attachment

$12 .... Ingredients (ricotta, Parmesan, eggs, sauce, etc.)

$19 ....Pandemic-proof gloves and mask

Well, OK, the math will probably work out in the long run; after all, you have to spend money to make money, right?

Turns out, I only need to make 172 pounds of assorted pasta to break even (if someone donates the ricotta)...*OR SOONER*, if Vons dramatically raises their spaghetti and ravioli prices.

It is now a beautiful Sunday afternoon. Martha is having an absolutely relaxing time. She is sunning herself while reading a book on our patio, surrounded by bright flowers, soft music, and chirping birds.

I, on the other hand, find myself in a hot kitchen, up to my tushy in all-purpose flour and ricotta, looking like the Abominable Snowman, making my F#&^%$$&% eighty-seven dollars per pound raviolis.

Frankly, I'm over it, but I'm afraid that if I stop making pasta for one minute during any free time for the next year, *Martha will kill me.*

AMAZON UPDATE

Martha wanted to park in our garage again and made me recycle the tower of Amazon boxes in the way. Of course, as soon as the garbage truck turned the corner, I desperately needed a large box. What to do? Then it hit me. Simple: I ordered another battery from Amazon, and presto…next day, box.

Amazon starting early on our Christmas order

Neighbor's trash. Nice to know that we are not the only ones!

AMAZON WARS

Being together 24/7 for what seems like twenty years now has resulted in some weird dynamics between us. We have definitely entered a subtle and unspoken trend. I think we have started to compete for Amazon's attention. I truly believe that this is a diabolical plot initiated by our Alexa to drive sales.

It was well documented that I had wisely purchased a twenty-five-pound bag of flour.

Well, Martha retaliated with what must be a gallon of capers. So, I raised her a fifty-pound chocolate bar. *The ball is in her court.*

MORE OBSERVATIONS

Things are getting really weird.

Yesterday morning, I overheard Martha on the phone trading a no-longer-used baby seat for two spray bottles of cleanser.

That afternoon, I traded my sister-in-law two pairs of latex gloves for a dozen eggs.

I find myself no longer using the term "miles per gallon." I am on months per gallon.

We used to count squirrels on our walks; now we count delivery trucks.

Where my car used to be, once again stands a massive pyramid of Amazon boxes…'cause you never know when you will need that six-by-eight-foot box.

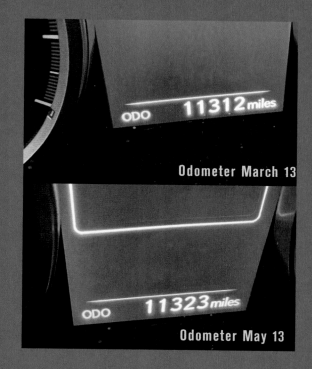

Odometer March 13

Odometer May 13

GROOMING DILEMMAS

All nail salons and barbershops have closed. By now, Martha is in a state of utter panic and desperate for a pedicure. SO, *WHOM DOES SHE TURN TO?* Yes, me...*SHAKY JOHNNY*, the one with Parkinson's. She claims that she can't reach her toes and in no way can she cut her own nails...

I finally relent and attempt a pedicure... pretty jagged result...but I am proud that no blood was shed that night.

Now, I need *my* toes clipped and Martha seems like my only option. Knowing that in fifty years of marriage, my Princess Bride had never touched a nail clipper, I am somewhat reluctant (read: *terrified*) to have her return the favor.

At least *I* know my way around a nail clipper, having cut my own nails for seventy of my seventy-three years on this planet. Throughout those decades, I proudly stuck to the righteous mantra: "REAL MEN DON'T GET PEDICURES."

However, cutting my own toenails became dangerous at about seventy. With balance, shaking, and short arm issues, I began to accept my inevitable fate. I was finally going to give the "croissant and nail salon" crowd a try. After all, how traumatic could a three-minute activity be?

TOE TRUCK

Well, I should have been tipped off right away when the name was Stella's Nail Salon and not Joe's Nail Cutting Place... add twenty dollars for a fancy-sounding place. Then, did you know, cuticles are a thing? Add fifteen dollars for taking care of those. Then, to stretch this three-minute service into a forty-five-dollar experience, you are handed a menu. Your nail cutter/consultant/torturer immediately starts up-selling you with much enthusiasm, pointing excitedly to the seventy-five-dollar ULTIMATE EXTRAVAGANZA PACKAGE. I finally point to something on the menu, if for no other reason than to get back to the soap that I am now involved in on the giant TV.

Turns out I pointed to a "Deluxe Leg Massage," an extremely painful leg pounding that seems to last hours. By now, I am screaming in my head, "Make it stop," but since I am the only male in a sea of smiling women in some kind of peaceful trance, I resist the urge to grab my sandals and make a run for it. Once the ordeal is over, I am grateful to fork over my seventy-five dollars (cash only) and actually start looking forward to my next beating. I do get more for my money than most clients, with poor Stella having to spend three-fourths of the session chasing my bouncy Parkinson toes all over her pristine towels.

But, I have totally digressed from my original toenail plight.

My plan was to wait this dilemma out till California opened again. Surely, by the time my toes poked through my slippers, Stella would be pounding legs again.

But no such luck. This week, my big toe accomplished its mission of burrowing through both my right sock and slipper. I became depressed, facing an inevitable choice. Not even the small googly eyes glued on my protruding toe could cheer me up anymore.

It therefore came down to Martha or using my precious miles to fly to a liberated state like Georgia where there were no Covid-related restrictions. Martha won out.

Now, I don't want to say she did a bad job, *but that woman is not getting anywhere near my hair with a pair of scissors!*

EXERCISE PROGRAM UPDATE

I was so pleased with my new hand weights, that I ordered a Pilates ball from the same catalog.*

Unimpressed with my unconventional weight loss approaches, Martha took matters into her own hands and put me on the extreme NO MAS diet.

*I must confess that I gave the hand weights only a one-star review due to how often they need to be reordered and a lack of volume discounts.

PILL MAGIC

I can no longer open a pill bottle without at least three occupants making a run for it. One falls on my foot, I look down, and it's gone…forever. If you have linoleum, you will go blind staring at the pattern. If you have carpeting, forget about it, they are chameleons changing on the way down to match the color of the carpet.

The real culprit, though, is a hardwood floor. The little critters generate so much speed when they hit the ground that they can reach the refrigerator from anywhere in the house. They slide under that sucker like they're heading for home plate at Yankee Stadium. This is why we actually use the undercarriage of our refrigerator as an emergency backup pharmacy.

DAILY DECISIONS

We have to cope with many more complicated issues. For example:

Someone is walking toward you (say, one thousand feet away), and you start doing the math...Should I cross the street? If so, when should I cross? Should I play chicken with the person and see who breaks first? Wait, they're not wearing a mask...*RUN!*

It is a fairly easy decision when no one is on the other side of the street.

BUT, this morning, a landscaper was walking toward me with a lawn mower, and at the same speed on the other side was a woman pushing a stroller. The landscaper and the baby were wearing a mask...but not the mother...HAAAAAAAAA, I turned around and ran home.

SMART APPLIANCE WARS

I think the next war will not be with China or any other country. It is going to be with our appliances. They are getting way too smart, and I believe they are coming for us. Not that we don't deserve it—we have been mistreating and abusing them for decades. How would you like to be this great history-changing microwave oven and only be used to heat coffee? Or be this proud refrigerator and never have your underneath cleaned till the family moves? Don't even get me going on our treatment of vacuum cleaners...but I digress.

My suspicion/paranoia is actually based on fact. Last night, at 1:00 a.m., I awoke to the sound of loud, strange voices downstairs. I grabbed my slipper for a weapon and tippy-toed down the stairs and around the corner (thank goodness for my pedicure keeping me from clicking noisily across the floor)...but I digress again. This is when I caught my smart TV ordering a pizza on Amazon using Alexa. True story...well, except for the pizza part; I am not sure that it was a pizza order because the TV went dark before I could find the right remote. By then, my upstairs iPad had warned the TV over Bluetooth that I was coming down.

MILEAGE UPDATE

As you may recall, last month, my very smart watch announced its approval of my walking thirty-six miles. Of course, thirty of those miles were walking from the couch to the refrigerator and back. That is when Martha put me on the extreme NO MAS diet.

I was therefore surprised when my watch blared another pride bulletin: this time for forty-four miles. I was perplexed because I have grown so fond of my jammies (and so weak from my diet) that I had not gone out much.

I dug deep into the analysis app and discovered the following breakdown:

- One mile walking to the mailbox

- Four miles checking if the refrigerator was back

- Six miles checking for Amazon deliveries

- Four miles in a figure eight pattern around the living room and kitchen looking for the remote

- Six miles going to a room or closet…just to stand there trying to remember why I am there

- Three miles looking for my reading glasses

- Two miles looking for the book I have been reading for the past eighteen months

- Two miles looking for my ringing cell phone

- Five miles looking for my silenced cell phone

- Two miles looking for pills under furniture

- Nine miles looking for Martha

SMARTWATCH WARS

I bought a smartwatch, mainly to remind me when to take the plethora of pills I am now taking. My three-month supply of DOPA now comes in a tube the length of my arm.

First, let me say that without this watch I would probably never take a pill. I would truly recommend one to anybody having to remember more than one pill a day. There are a great variety of watches available, and each one performs differently.

I chose the Nike sports model, which sounded great. It keeps track of your vitals and calls your relatives if you fall down, think about falling down, or sneeze too hard. Over time, though, we developed a classic love-hate relationship. I am starting to TRULY dislike this watch and its authoritarian personality. I find myself constantly screaming:

"STOP, YOU'RE NOT THE BOSS OF ME!"

The watch is so annoying with its constant whining:

"You did much better yesterday."

"I bet your fellow boxers are already exercising with Mike."

"You did not meet any of your goals today; go to your room."

"You better take that pill right now, or I'll ring Martha's watch."

"Don't make me call her!"

"I smell beef—is that hamburger? Go ahead, have a heart attack; I know your heart rate."

ON, and on and on and on.

I am seriously thinking of trading it in for the SLOTH, COMPLIMENTARY MODEL. It seems to be so chill.

"I'm so sorry; did I wake you? I'll check back later."

"WOW, that cheeseburger smells good. Don't worry about your heart; we're probably OK."

"So, are we doing anything today? Totally cool if we don't."

"You are really fast, Johnny."

"You shut off the alarm and missed a pill…you are so naughty."

"Who's a good boy? You are—yes, you are."

JUNE OBSERVATIONS

Only two of us live here. So, how can our sink be like this every morning?

Every two weeks, on Sunday night, I religiously do two things:

1. I take at least two hours out of my busy schedule (divided equally between Netflix and napping) to carefully fill my two-week pill dispenser.

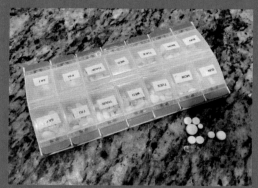

2. I strategically place pairs of reading glasses throughout the house (every six feet) so I can always locate a pair.

So, why is it that after two weeks, I always have fifteen extra pills and cannot find one ####&&#### pair of glasses anywhere?

LIGHTS OUT

Martha and I no longer use a ladder from fear of heights, vertigo, falling, shaking the thing for a Parkinson ride across the floor, etc. It is becoming a problem while we are still under quarantine and therefore shunned by all of our tall friends.

We have ten-foot ceilings, and even with Martha standing on my shoulders, we are still about four feet short of reaching our light bulbs. We are down to one bulb on our chandelier, and the ones in the kitchen are going fast.

I am afraid that it is going to be lights out if this lockdown lasts more than another couple of weeks.

AMAZON UPDATE

We achieved a personal best over the weekend. I keep looking outside expecting Jeff Bezos to hop out of the next delivery truck and personally thank us. This lockdown is getting very expensive.

Also, Martha has been warning me that if I do not shape up, she will ship me out. I paid little attention, but the only box she is saving is worrisome.

JULY OBSERVATIONS

1. I think I am losing my hearing. I base this on a recent conversation with the lovely Martha:

   Martha from living room: John, did you put the pizza in the oven?

   John from office: What?

   Martha: I said, did you put the pizza in the oven?

   John: You want a pizza oven?

   Martha: No, I SAID, DID YOU put the pizza in the oven?

   John: What? CAN'T HEAR YOU.

   Martha at top of lungs: DID YOU PUT THE ©ƒ©ƒgbbʃ¢£££££ pizza in the F&^^%%$$## oven?

   John: OK, OK, I'll order one on Amazon.

2. Companies are making more cold calls as their stores are shut down. I got a call from Apple wanting to know if I had heard that their latest laptop would cut my workload in half…so, I ordered two.

CRUSHING THE CURVE

As a result of flattening my weight curve for three weeks, Martha eliminated the main Phase I restriction and had our refrigerator brought back.

Then, she liberated me to Phase II.

SQUIRREL WARS

In preparation for the worsening conflict with the squirrels, I turned to Amazon and found these products...all available by next day delivery.

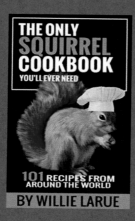

Squirrel caller

The delivery box can be recycled as a live trap

UNFORESEEN CONSEQUENCES

EXERCISE AND ACTIVITIES UPDATE

When Martha does not want to take John for his walk yet still wants to exercise him…

As time marches on with the pandemic still raging, John and Martha find new ways to entertain themselves.

FINAL OBSERVATION

For the past ten years, my children have waged war on my grandchildren trying to limit their screen time. Now, with home and remote education, their positions have reversed. The parents are now begging the kids to quit hiding their iPads and do their homework.

BREAKTHROUGH HYPNOSIS SESSION

John recalls how he just stood there frozen during the tragic event resulting in his mistrust of squirrels.

Unfortunately, the lights did not outlast the lockdown.

Martha?

John?

LIBERATION

After five long months, California reopened the trails and some businesses. We assumed a return to a normal life going forward...WRONG!

Goodwill center opens.

I saw two humans yesterday.
Today, I saw four.
I think they're multiplying

Ya, something about a second wave

A college professor once pleaded with John Pistacchi to become a writer. John, sensing more money in software, started a successful Silicon Valley computer firm instead. However, his professor's words never faded, and John dabbled in publishing throughout his career. He has published articles in *Reader's Digest* and in-flight magazines for American Airlines.

His retirement has enabled him to return to his old passion. Since the beginning of the COVID-19 lockdown, John has been posting weekly observations of the humorous side of the lockdown as a way of keeping in touch with his Parkinson's boxing group till the gym reopens. This book—an accumulation of those weekly musings—is his latest attempt at extending his literary career while maintaining his sanity in these insane times through a self-depreciating sense of humor.

Made in the USA
Las Vegas, NV
06 March 2021